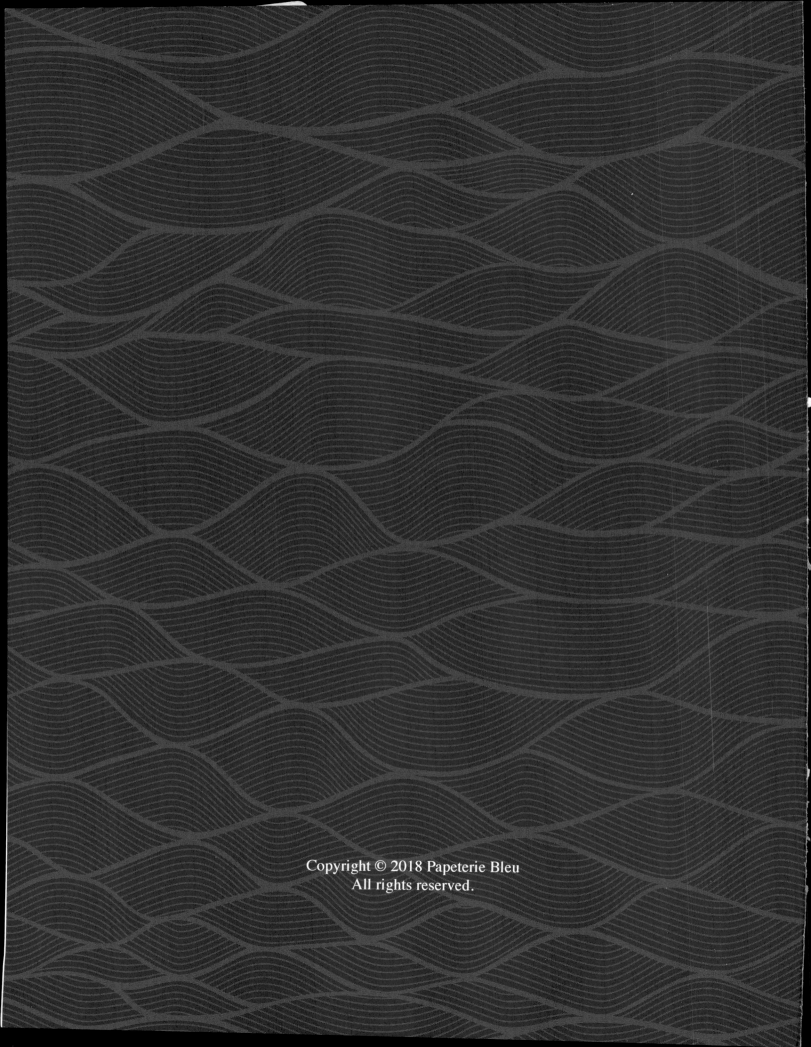

FREE DOWNLOAD

www.papeteriebleu.com/swim

YOUR DOWNLOAD CODE: SWM935

@papeteriebleu

Papeterie Bleu

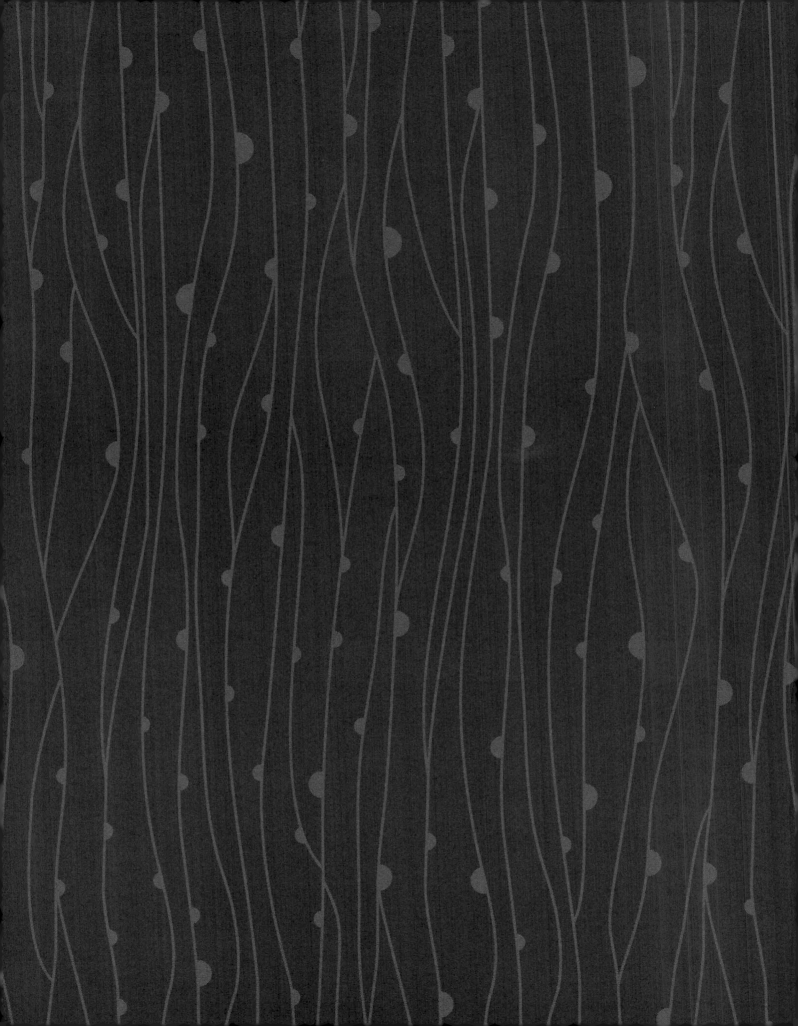

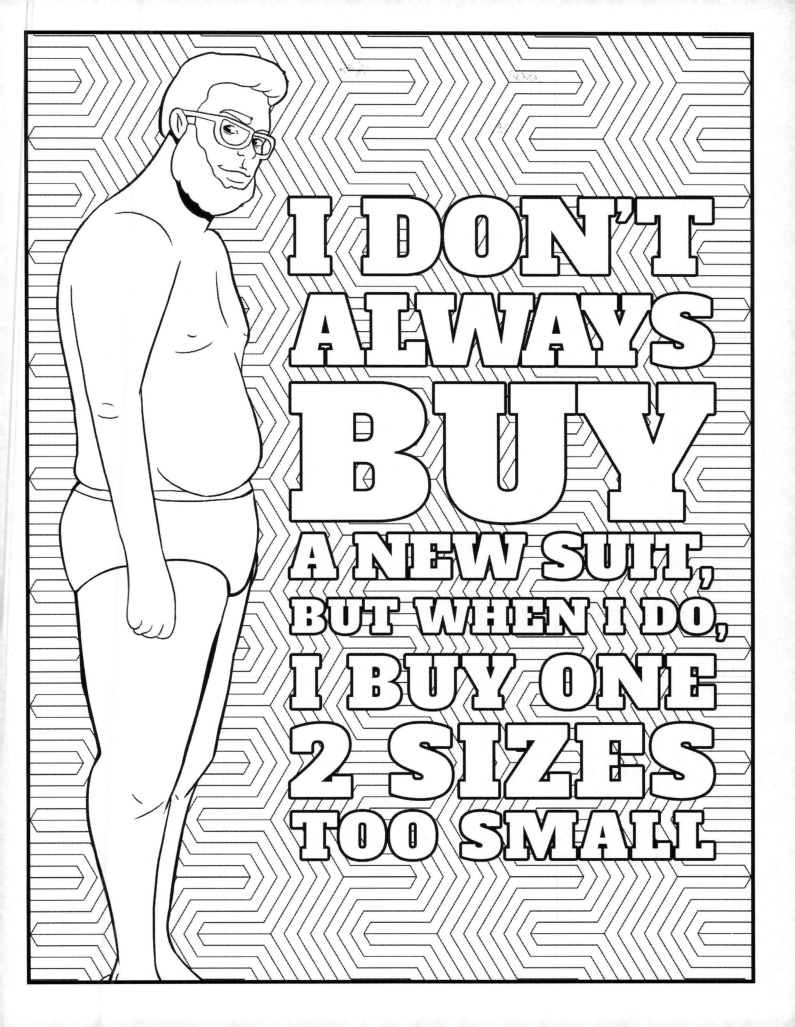

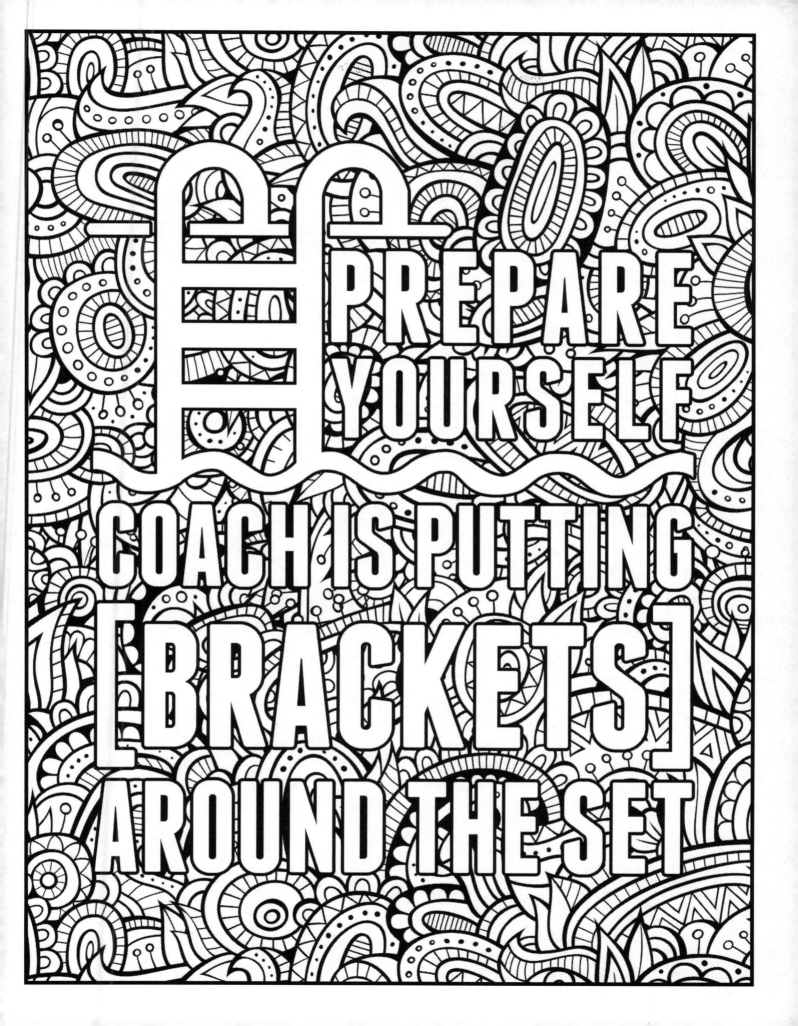

PREPARE YOURSELF

COACH IS PUTTING

[BRACKETS]

AROUND THE SET

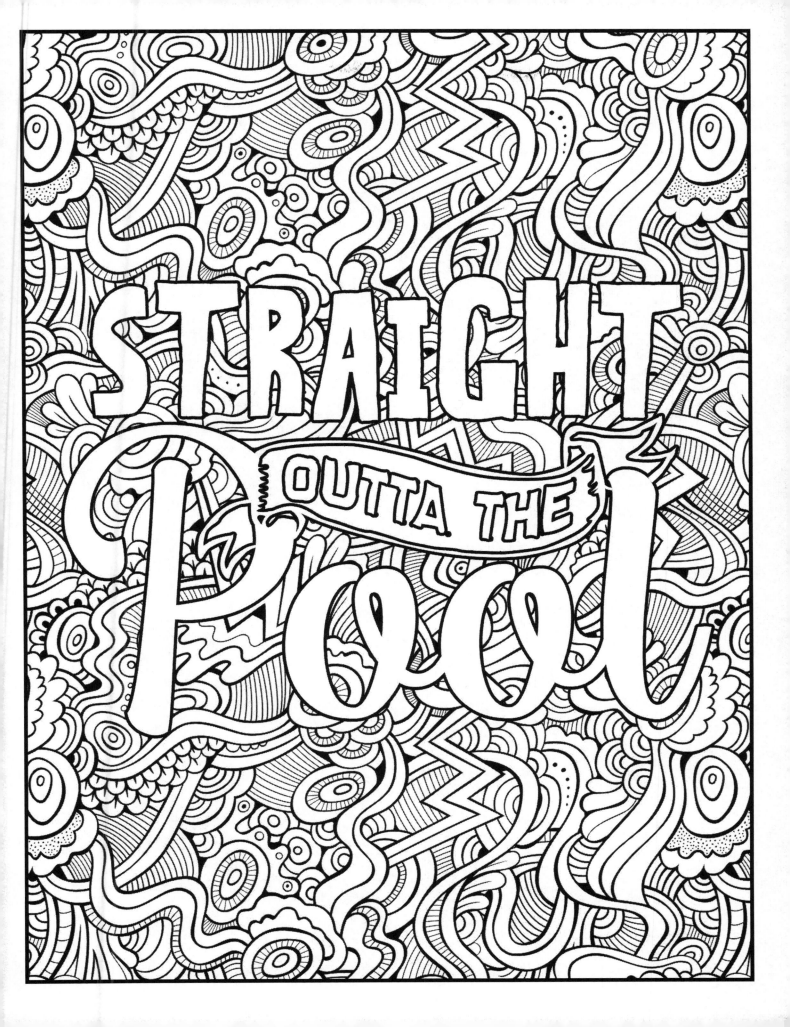

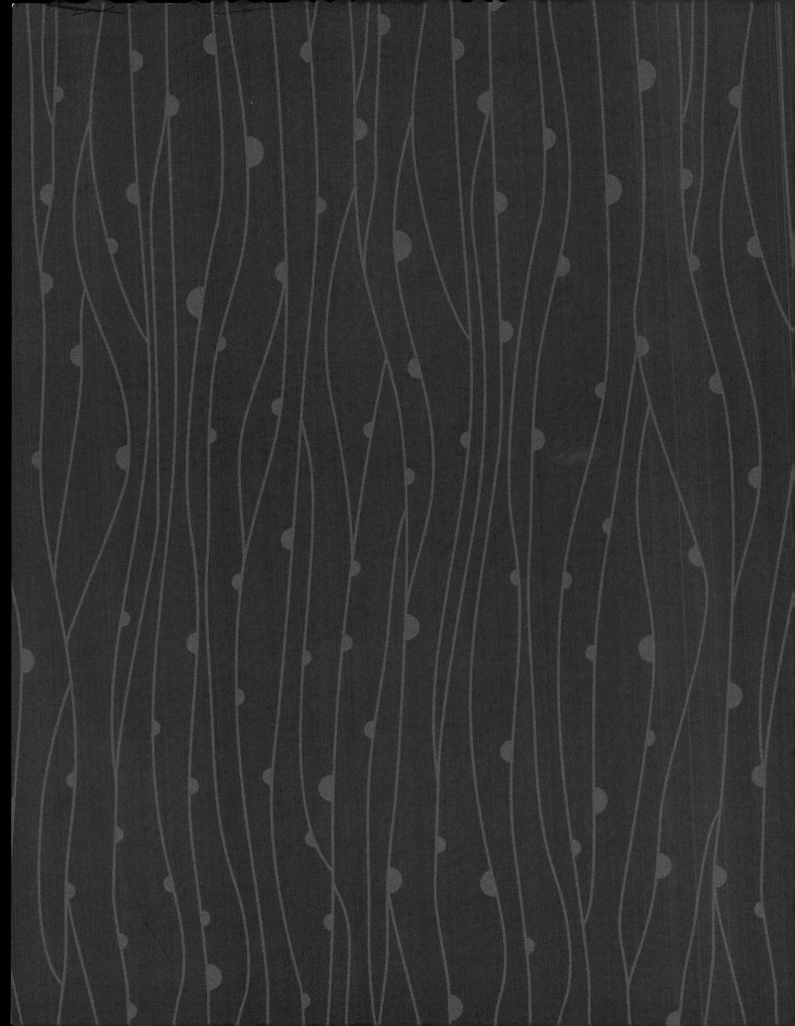

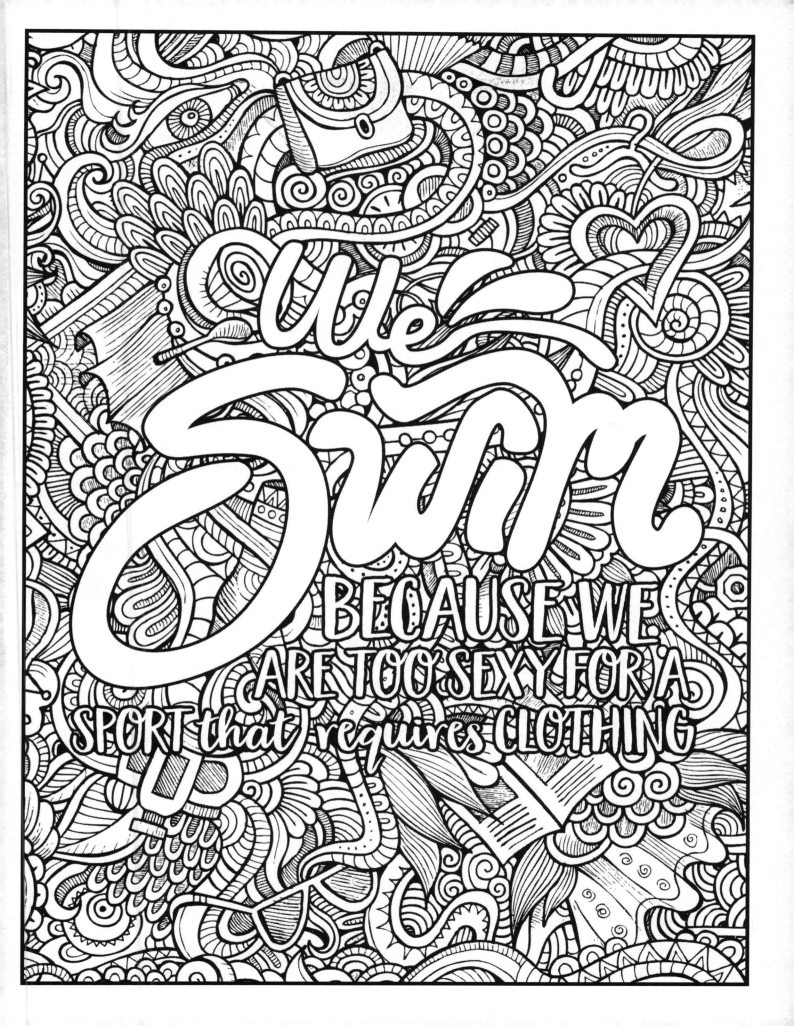

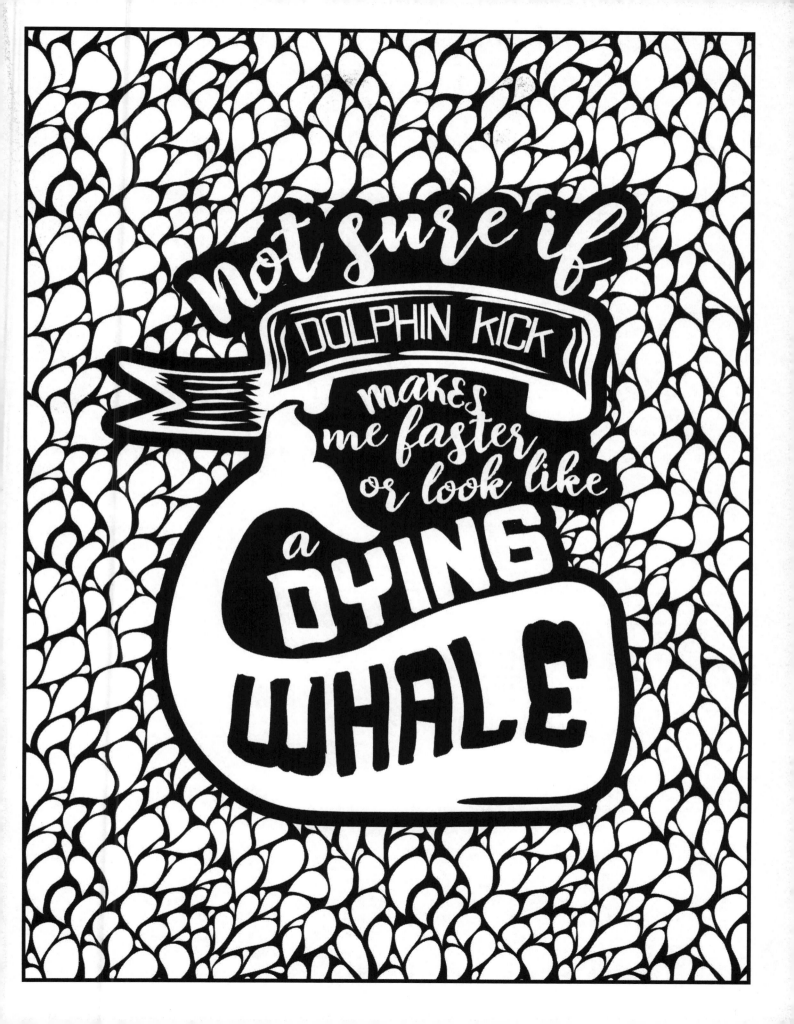

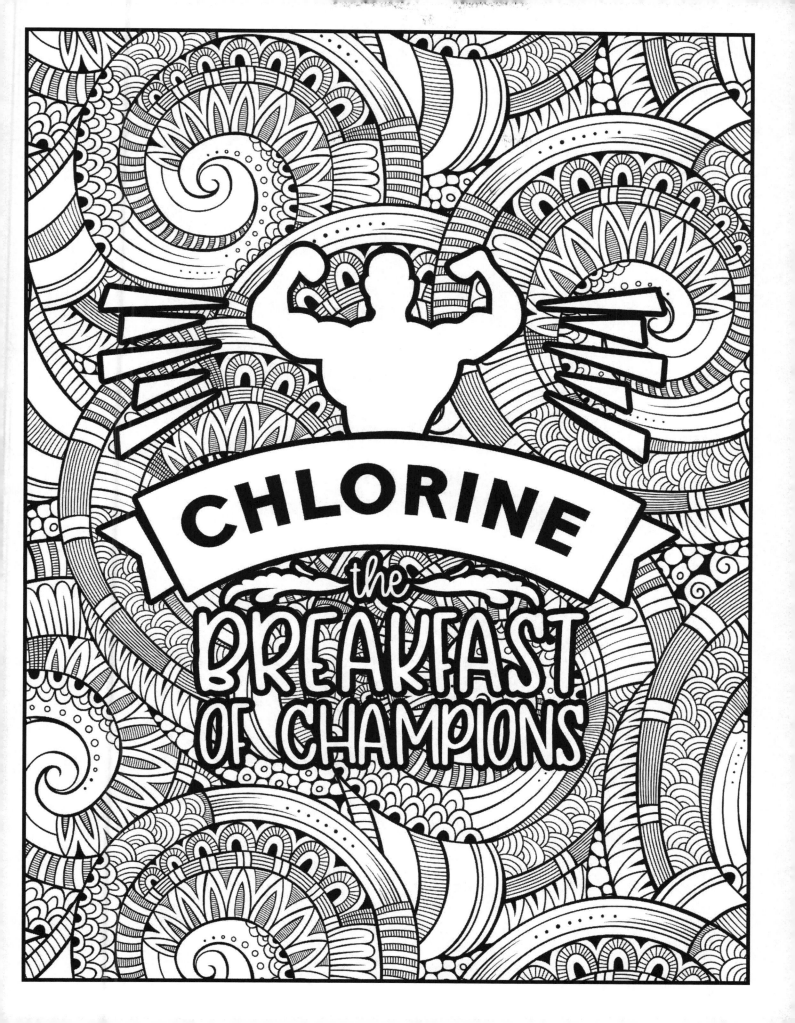

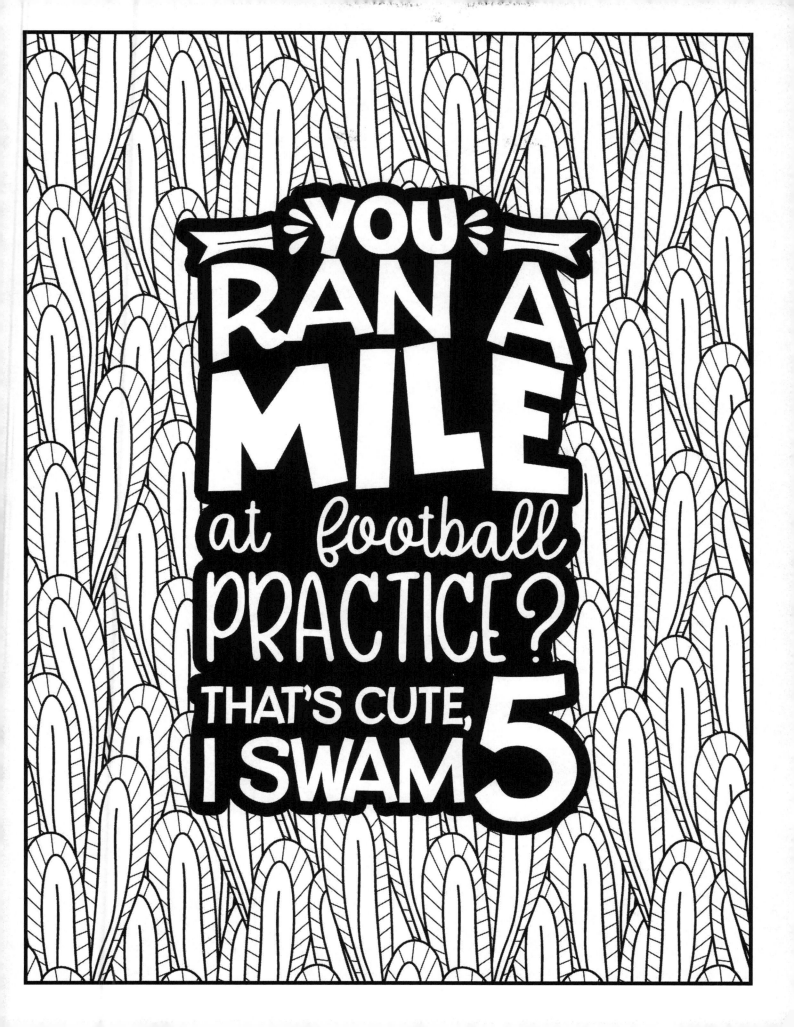

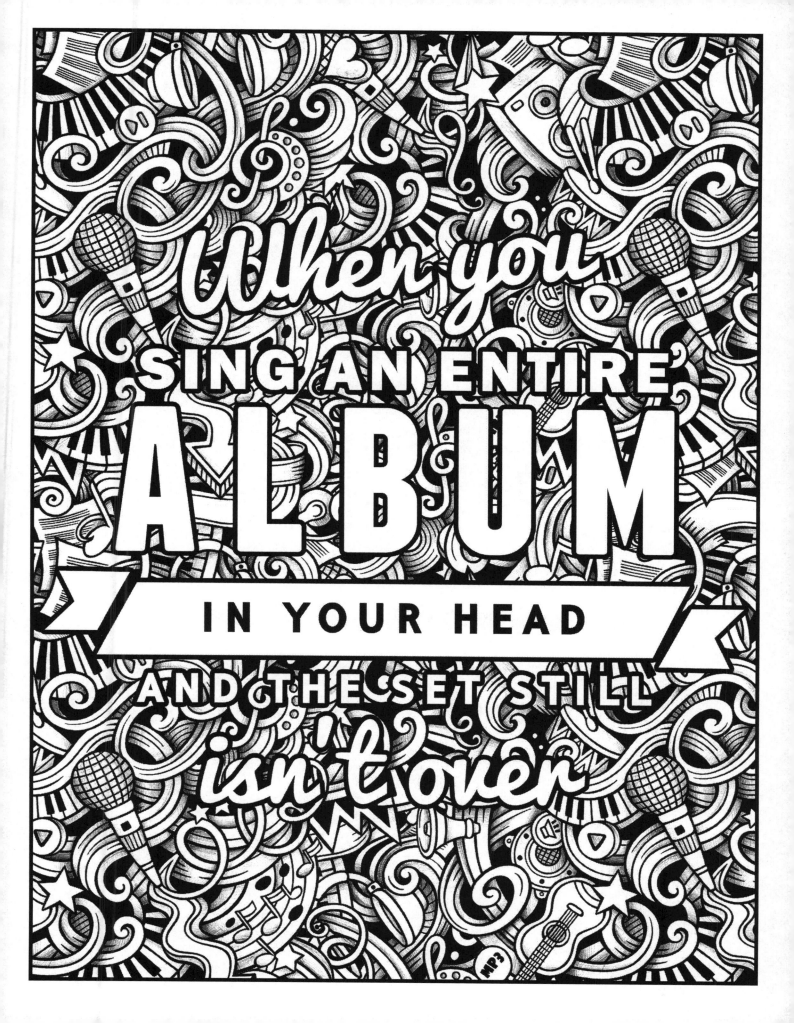

Happiness is not Having to set an alarm for TOMORROW

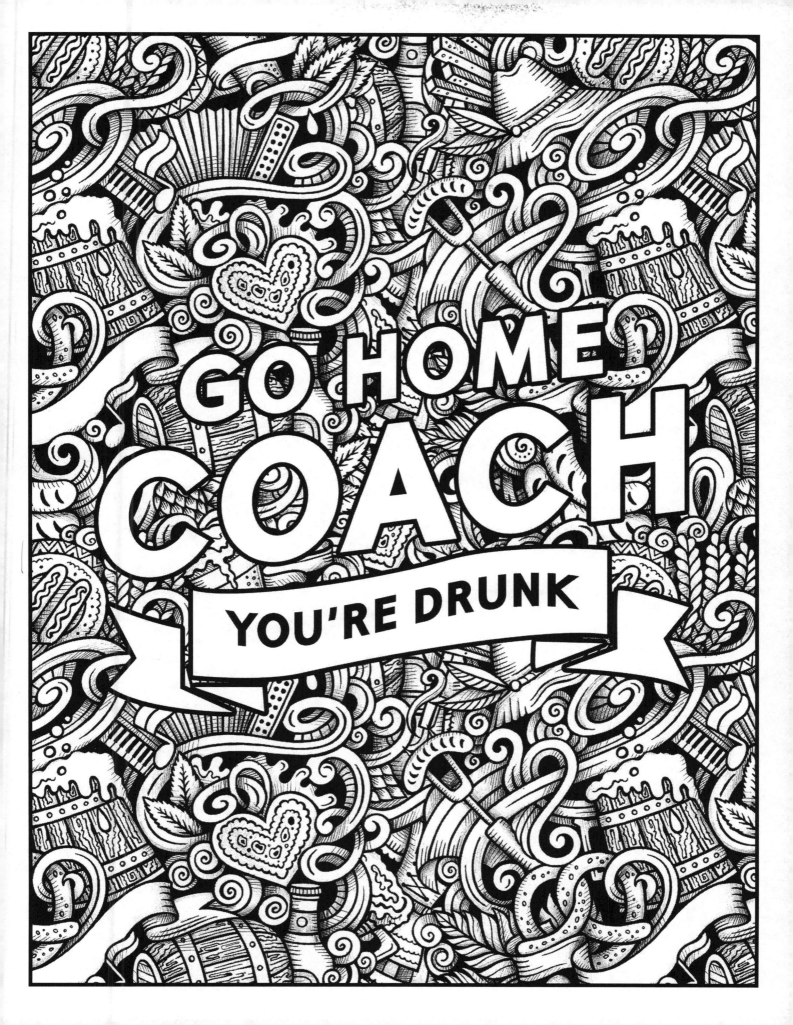

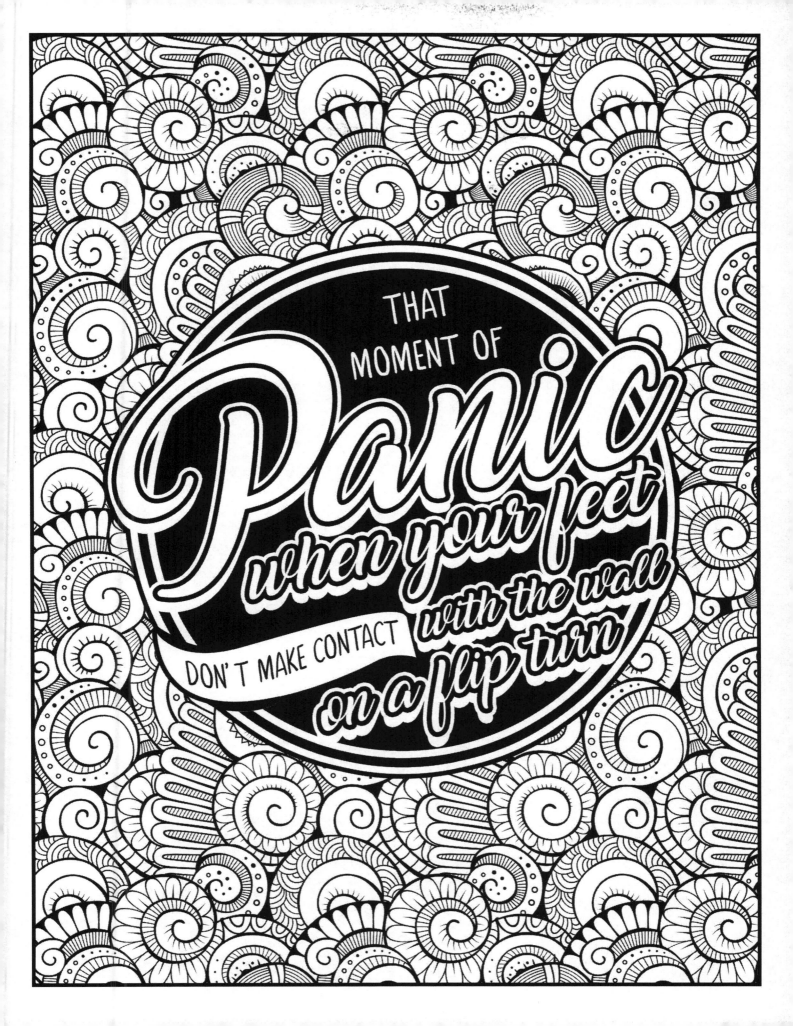

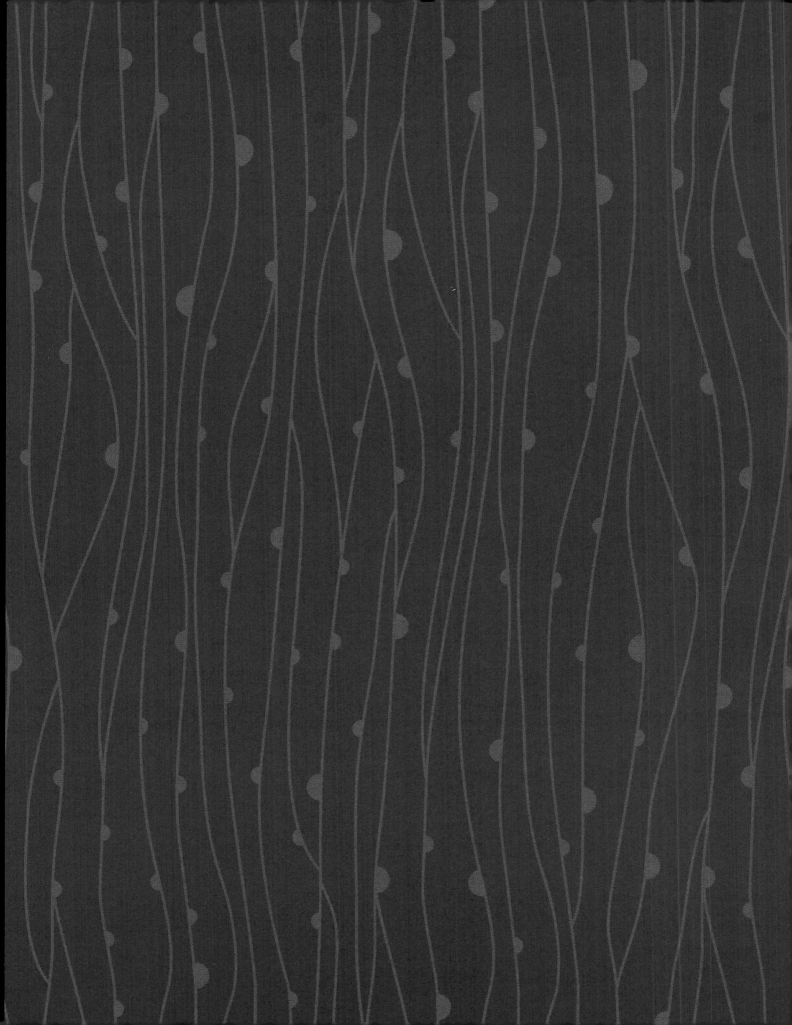

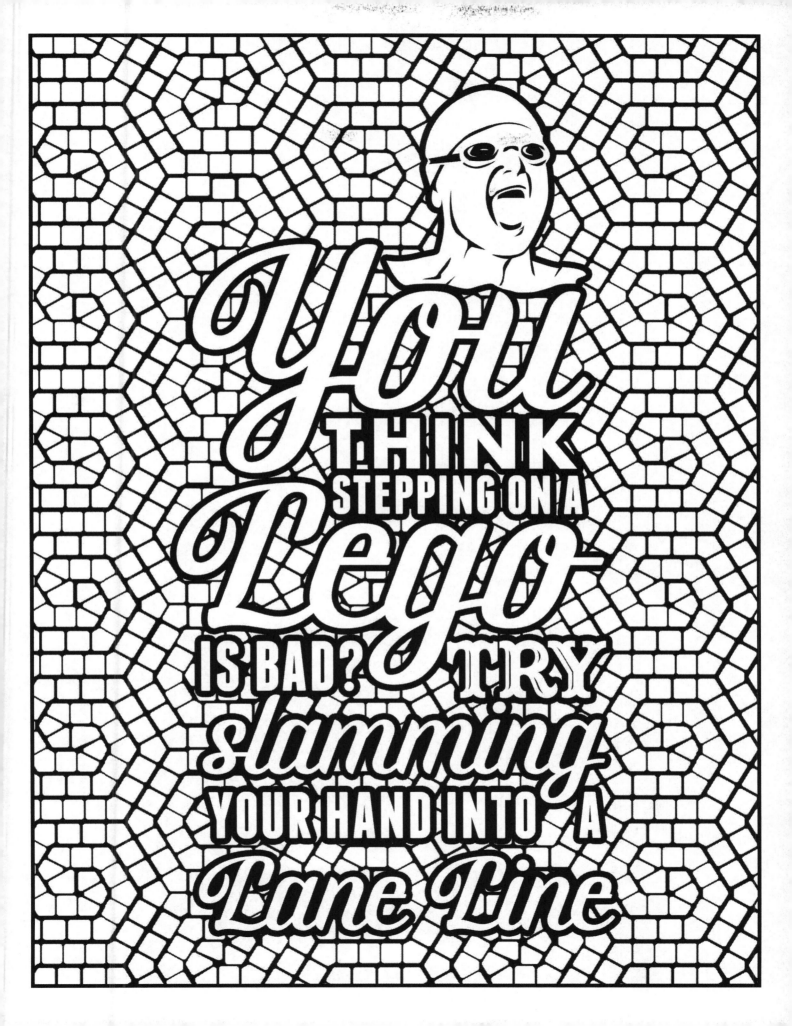

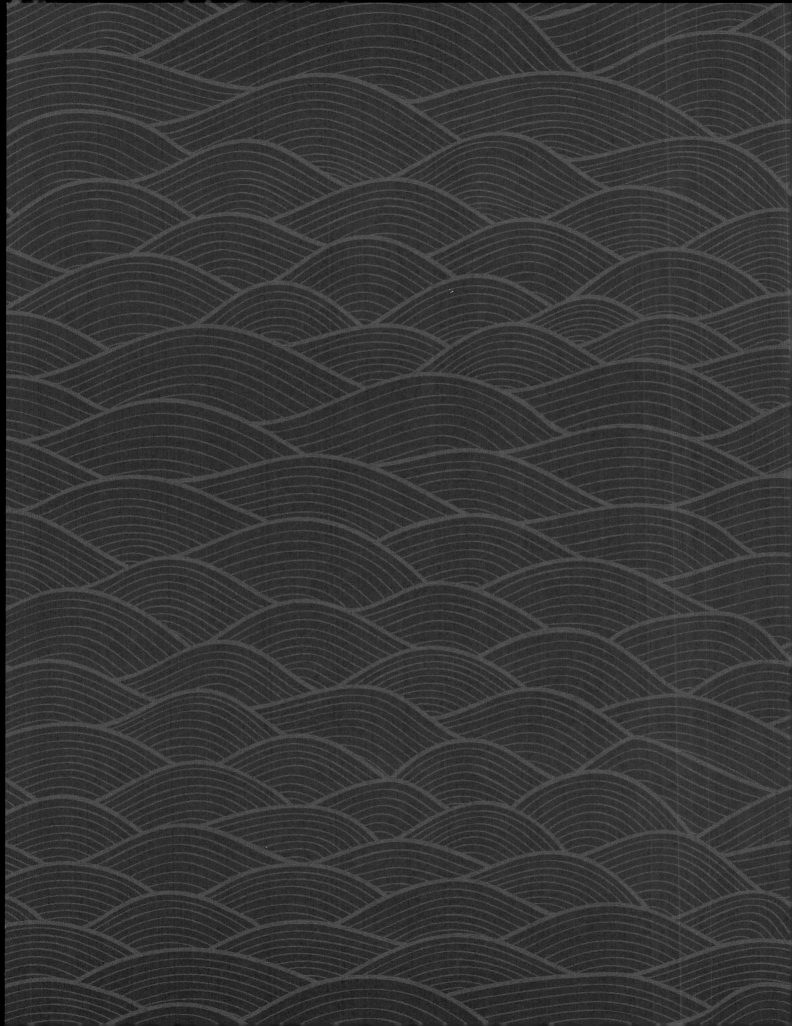

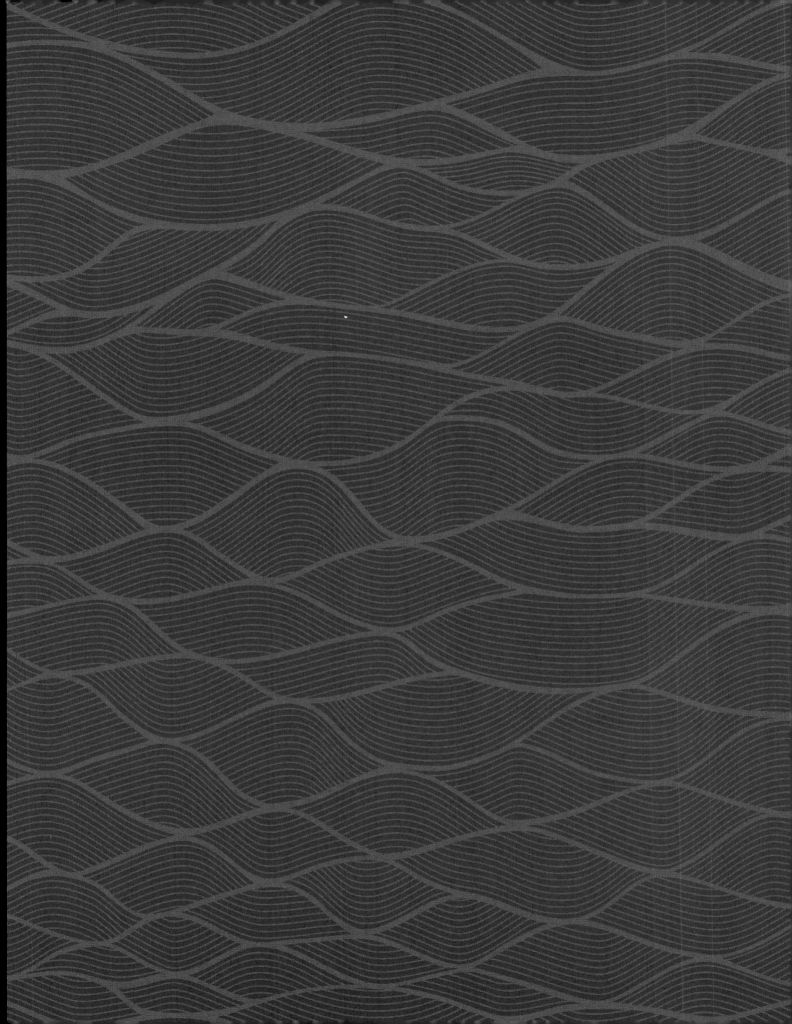

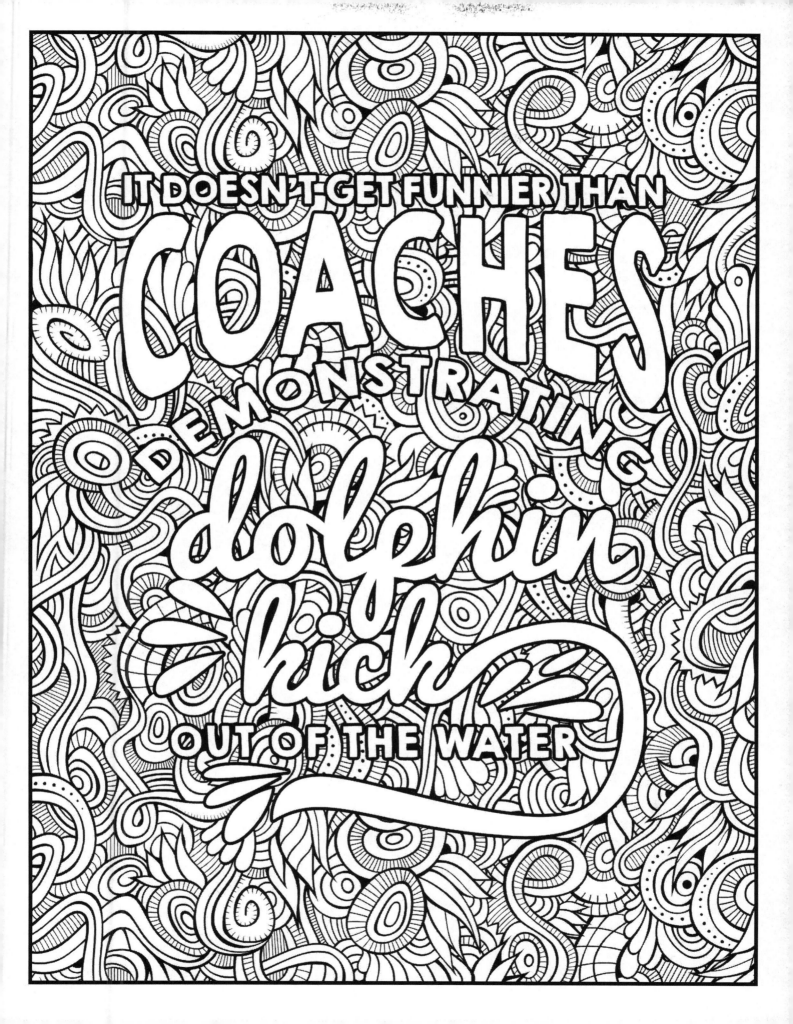

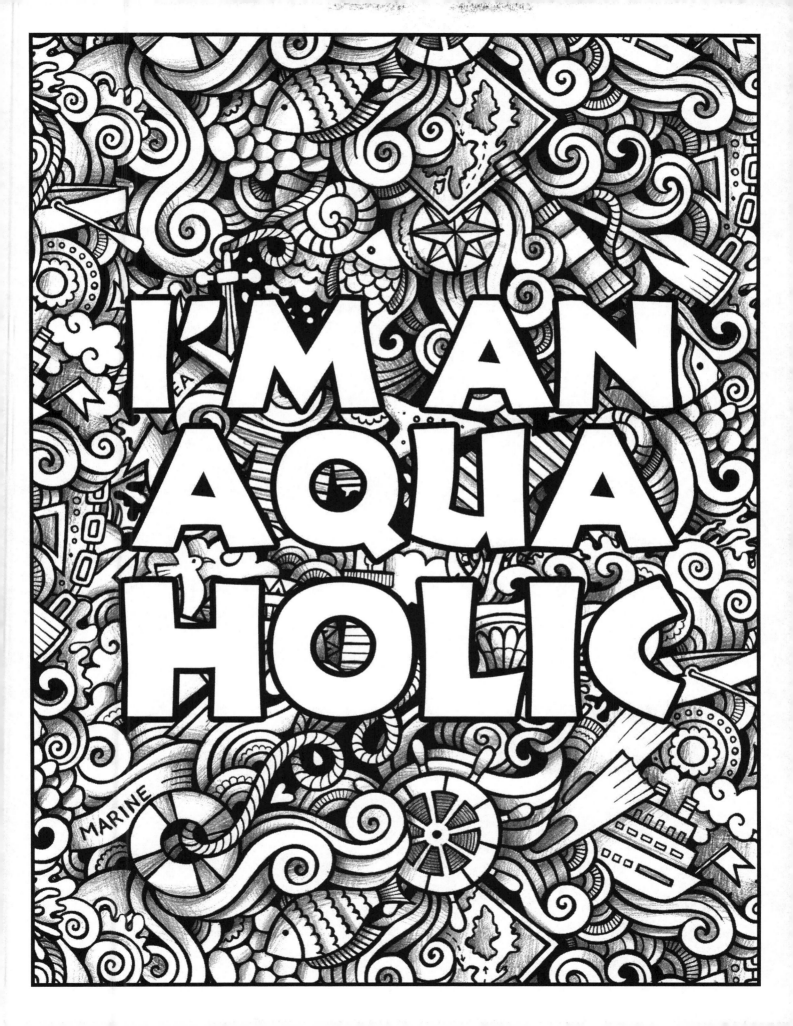

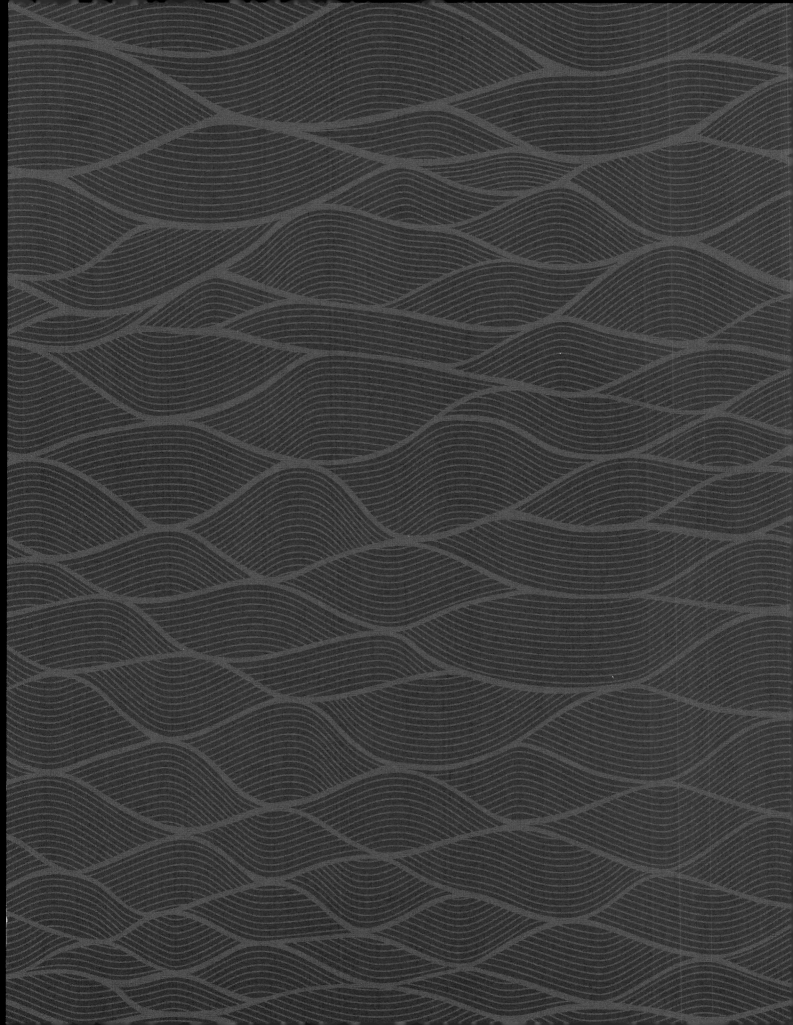

BE SURE TO FOLLOW US ON SOCIAL MEDIA FOR THE LATEST NEWS, SNEAK PEEKS, & GIVEAWAYS

@PapeterieBleu

Papeterie Bleu

@PapeterieBleu

ADD YOURSELF TO OUR MONTHLY NEWSLETTER FOR FREE DIGITAL DOWNLOADS AND DISCOUNT CODES

www.papeteriebleu.com/newslette

#BEERLIFE
SNARKY ADULT COLORING BOOK FOR BEER LOVERS

#OFFICELIFE
A SNARKY COLORING BOOK FOR ADULTS

NO COFFEE NO WERKEE

#VETLIFE
A SNARKY ADULT COLORING BOOK

#VETTECHLIFE
A SNARKY ADULT COLORING BOOK

#DOCTORLIFE
A SNARKY ADULT COLORING BOOK

#TEACHERLIFE
SNARKY CHALKBOARD COLORING BOOK

#NURSELIFE
A SNARKY ADULT COLORING BOOK

#MOMLIFE
A SNARKY ADULT COLORING BOOK

MAMA HAIR DON'T CARE

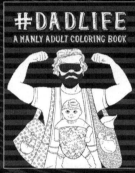

#DADLIFE
A MANLY ADULT COLORING BOOK

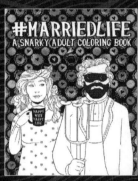

#MARRIEDLIFE
A SNARKY ADULT COLORING BOOK

HAPPY WIFE HAPPY LIFE

SWIMMERLIFE
SNARKY ADULT COLORING BOOK

CHLORINE HAIR DON'T CARE

DÍA DE LOS MUERTOS
SUGAR SKULL COLORING BOOK

DÍA DE LOS PERROS
DOG SUGAR SKULL COLORING BOOK

MASTER MANDALAS
an ADULT COLORING BOOK

MINDFUL MANDALAS
an ADULT COLORING BOOK

UGH. I CAN'T EVEN.
MANDALAS? MEH.
SNARKY ADULT COLORING BOOK

MANDALAS FOR MEDITATION
A MANDALA COLORING BOOK

EVERYONE IS THE WORST
MORE MANDALAS?!? UGH.
A SNARKY MANDALA COLORING BOOK

WONDERLAND
A FANTASY ADULT COLORING BOOK

be FEARLESS in the pursuit of WHAT sets YOUR soul on fire
AN INSPIRATIONAL COLOURING BOOK FOR EVERYONE

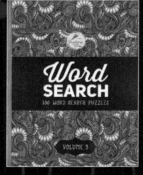
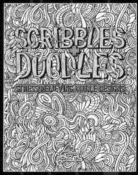

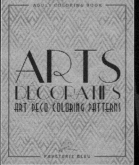

Made in the USA
Middletown, DE
12 February 2020